BRAZIL 2016 HUMAN RIGHTS REPORT

EXECUTIVE SUMMARY

Brazil is a constitutional, multiparty republic. In 2014 voters re-elected Dilma Rousseff as president in elections widely considered free and fair. On August 31, Rousseff was impeached, and Vice President Michel Temer assumed the presidency as required by the constitution.

Civilian authorities at times did not maintain effective control over security forces.

The most significant human rights abuses included excessive force and unlawful killings by state police, poor and at times life-threatening conditions in some prisons, and corruption.

Other human rights problems included beatings, abuse, and torture of detainees and inmates by police and prison security forces; prolonged pretrial detention and inordinate delays of trials; judicial censorship of media; violence and discrimination against women and girls; violence against children, including sexual abuse; sex trafficking, including of children; social conflict between indigenous communities and private landowners that occasionally led to violence; discrimination against indigenous persons and minorities; violence and social discrimination against lesbian, gay, bisexual, transgender, and intersex persons; violence against environmentalists and rural workers; exploitative working conditions, including forced labor and child labor in the informal economy and in parts of the formal economy; and inadequate enforcement of labor laws.

The government prosecuted officials who committed abuses; however, an inefficient judicial process delayed justice for perpetrators as well as survivors.

Section 1. Respect for the Integrity of the Person, Including Freedom from:

a. Arbitrary Deprivation of Life and other Unlawful or Politically Motivated Killings

There were no reports the federal government or its agents committed politically motivated killings, but unlawful killings by state police occurred. In some cases police employed indiscriminate force. The extent of the problem was difficult to determine, as comprehensive, reliable statistics on unlawful police killings were not available. Official statistics showed police killed numerous civilians (lawfully

or unlawfully) in encounters each year. For instance, the Rio de Janeiro Public Security Institute, a state government entity, reported that from January to July, police killed 473 civilians in "acts of resistance" (similar to resisting arrest) in Rio de Janeiro State. Most of the deaths occurred while police were conducting operations against drug-trafficking gangs in the city of Rio de Janeiro's approximately 760 favelas (poor neighborhoods or shantytowns), where an estimated 1.4 million persons lived. A disproportionate number of the victims were Afro-Brazilians under age 25. Nongovernmental organizations (NGOs) in Rio de Janeiro questioned whether all of the victims actually resisted arrest, contending police continued to employ repressive methods. In April police conducted an operation in Acari, a favela in the city of Rio de Janeiro, that resulted in the deaths of five civilians. Official reports showed the casualties took place during an intense shootout, but residents of the community claimed police summarily executed the victims. Residents also reported problems of excessive use of force by police during the operation. As of November the case was under investigation. A report by the NGO Amnesty International, *A Legacy of Violence-- Killings by Police and Repression of Protests at Rio 2016*, noted violent police operations took place throughout the Olympic Games (August 5-21) in several poor communities of Rio de Janeiro, resulting in the deaths of at least eight persons. On August 11, a 19-year-old man was killed during a joint operation involving civil and military police agents, the army, and the National Security Force in the favela of Complexo da Mare. On the same day, police officers from the Riot Police Unit killed two children ages 14 and 15 and a man age 22 in the Bandeira 2 favela, in the neighborhood of Del Castilho. On August 15, officers from the Pacification Police Unit killed a man in the favela of Cantagalo, in Ipanema. The next day civil police killed three men during an operation in the favela of Complexo da Mare.

In February, nine officers from the Bahia state military police Special Patrolling Group were implicated in the killing of 12 young Afro-Brazilians in Cabula, a neighborhood in the state capital of Salvador. Police and autopsy reports indicated the victims were unarmed and offered no resistance. Nevertheless, in July, Judge Marivalda Almeida Moutinho acquitted the nine of all charges, ruling the officers acted in self-defense.

b. Disappearance

There were no reports of politically motivated disappearances.

c. Torture and Other Cruel, Inhuman, or Degrading Treatment or Punishment

The constitution prohibits such treatment and provides severe legal penalties for conviction of its use. There were, nevertheless, cases of degrading treatment such as those documented by Juan Mendez, UN special rapporteur on torture and other cruel, inhuman, or degrading treatment or punishment, who visited the country in August 2015 and published his findings in January. Credible testimony from inmates--women, men, girls, and boys chosen at random in various detention facilities--pointed to the frequent use of torture and mistreatment, varying in methods and the severity of the pain and suffering inflicted. The incidents occurred during arrest and interrogation by police and also while inmates were in the custody of prison personnel. The inmates reported police and prison personnel engaged in severe kicking, beating (sometimes with sticks and truncheons), and suffocation. Inmates also reported police and prison personnel used Taser guns, pepper spray, tear gas, noise bombs, and rubber bullets, as well as profuse verbal abuse and threats.

Prison and Detention Center Conditions

Conditions in many prisons were poor and sometimes life threatening mainly due to overcrowding. Abuse by prison guards, including sexual abuse, continued at many facilities, and poor working conditions and low pay for prison guards encouraged corruption.

<u>Physical Conditions</u>: Endemic overcrowding was a problem. According to the Ministry of Justice and Citizenship, as of November the prison population was 711,463 prisoners (including house arrests); the official capacity of the prison system was 376,669 prisoners. According to the Catholic Church's Penitentiary Commission, in some states women were occasionally held with men, although in separate cells. Prisoners who committed petty crimes frequently were held with murderers and other violent criminals. Authorities attempted to hold pretrial detainees separately from convicted prisoners, but lack of space often required holding convicted criminals in pretrial detention facilities. Many prisons, including in the Federal District, attempted to separate violent offenders from nonviolent ones and to keep convicted drug traffickers in a wing apart from the rest of the prison population. Multiple sources reported adolescents were jailed with adults in poor and crowded conditions. In many juvenile detention centers, the number of inmates greatly exceeded capacity.

Violence was rampant in several prison facilities in the Northeast. In addition to overcrowding, poor administration of the prison system, the presence of gangs, and corruption contributed to violence within the penitentiary system. In July criminal organizations organized prison riots and violent acts throughout prison facilities in the state of Rio Grande do Norte after the state government announced it would install cell-phone jammers at prison facilities. Authorities deployed more than 1,000 army troops after 107 prisoners escaped and burned several public buses. In October prison clashes between rival gangs killed at least 18 inmates in two penitentiaries in the states of Roraima and Rondonia, according to press reports.

The press reported on multiple riots and escapes in the Curado prison complex in the state of Pernambuco. In June judges from the Inter-American Court of Human Rights visited the Curado prison (previously named the Anibal Bruno prison) in relation to a case brought against the state of Pernambuco regarding alleged human rights violations. As part of the Inter-American Court case, Human Rights Watch and other NGOs cited inadequate sanitary conditions. HIV and tuberculosis rates in prisons were far higher than rates for the general population. The prevalence of tuberculosis in Pernambuco's prisons was reportedly 37 times that of the general population.

Administration: Prisoners and detainees had access to visitors; however, human rights observers reported some visitors complained of screening procedures that at times included invasive and unsanitary physical exams. State-level ombudsman offices and the federal Secretariat of Human Rights monitored prison and detention center conditions and investigated credible allegations of inhuman conditions.

Independent Monitoring: The government permitted monitoring by independent nongovernmental observers, including the International Committee of the Red Cross, United Nations, and Organization of American States.

Improvements: In the Pedrinhas complex in the state of Maranhao, authorities reduced the level of violence by incarcerating rival gang leaders in separate facilities and professionalizing the prison guards, converting them from private contractors to public employees.

d. Arbitrary Arrest or Detention

The law prohibits arbitrary arrest and detention and limits arrests to those caught in the act of committing a crime or arrested by order of a judicial authority; however, police at times did not respect this prohibition.

Role of the Police and Security Apparatus

The federal police force, operating under the Ministry of Justice and Citizenship, is a small, primarily investigative entity and plays a minor role in routine law enforcement. Most police forces are under the control of the states. There are two distinct units within the state police forces: the civil police, which performs an investigative role, and the military police, which is charged with maintaining law and order. Despite its name, the military police does not report to the Ministry of Defense. The law mandates that special police courts exercise jurisdiction over state military police except those charged with "willful crimes against life," primarily homicide. Police often were responsible for investigating charges of torture and excessive force carried out by fellow officers, although independent investigations increased. Delays in the special military police courts allowed many cases to expire due to statutes of limitations.

Civilian authorities generally maintained effective control over security forces, and the government has mechanisms in place to investigate and punish abuse and corruption; however, impunity and a lack of accountability for security forces remained a problem.

In Rio de Janeiro's favelas, so-called militia groups composed of off-duty and former law enforcement officers often took policing into their own hands. Many militia groups intimidated residents and conducted illegal activities such as extorting protection money and providing pirated utility services.

According to the Rio de Janeiro State Secretariat for Public Security, human rights courses were a mandatory component of training for entry-level military police officers. Officers for the state's favela pacification program (UPP) received additional human rights training. During the year the military police in Rio de Janeiro provided human rights training to 120 UPP officers.

Arrest Procedures and Treatment of Detainees

Unless a suspect is caught in the act of committing a crime, an arrest cannot be made without a warrant issued by a judicial official. Officials must advise suspects of their rights at the time of arrest or before taking them into custody for interrogation. The law prohibits use of force during an arrest unless the suspect attempts to escape or resists arrest. According to human rights observers, some detainees complained of physical abuse while being taken into police custody.

Authorities generally respected the constitutional right to a prompt judicial determination of the legality of detention. Detainees were informed promptly of the charges against them. The law permits provisional detention for up to five days under specified conditions during an investigation, but a judge may extend this period. A judge may also order temporary detention for an additional five days for processing. Preventive detention for an initial period of 15 days is permitted if police suspect a detainee may leave the area. The law does not provide for a maximum period for pretrial detention, which is decided on a case-by-case basis. If detainees are convicted, time in detention before trial is subtracted from their sentences. Defendants arrested in the act of committing a crime must be charged within 30 days of arrest. Other defendants must be charged within 45 days, although this period may be extended. Often the period for charging defendants had to be extended because of court backlogs. Bail was available for most crimes, and defendants facing charges for all but the most serious crimes have the right to a bail hearing. Prison authorities generally allowed detainees prompt access to a lawyer. Indigent detainees have the right to a lawyer provided by the state. Detainees also were allowed prompt access to family members.

Pretrial Detention: According to the National Council of Justice, prisons held approximately 250,000 persons in preventive detention.

Detainee's Ability to Challenge Lawfulness of Detention before a Court: Persons arrested or detained may challenge in court the legal basis for their detention and obtain prompt release and compensation if found to have ben unlawfully detained.

e. Denial of Fair Public Trial

The constitution provides for an independent judiciary, and the government generally respected judicial independence. Local NGOs, however, cited that corruption within the judiciary, especially at the local and state levels, remained a concern.

Trial Procedures

The constitution provides for the right to a fair public trial, and an independent judiciary generally enforced this right, although NGOs reported that in some rural regions--especially in cases involving land rights activists--police, prosecutors, and the judiciary were perceived to be more susceptible to external influences, including fear of reprisals. Investigations, prosecutions, and trials in these cases often were delayed.

After an arrest a judge reviews the case, determines whether it should proceed, and assigns the case to a state prosecutor, who decides whether to issue an indictment. Juries hear cases involving capital crimes; judges try those accused of lesser crimes. Defendants enjoy a presumption of innocence and have the right to be present at their trial, to be promptly informed of charges, not to be compelled to testify or confess guilt, to have access to government-held evidence and confront and question adverse witnesses, to present their own witnesses and evidence, and to appeal verdicts. The law extends these rights to all defendants. Defendants generally had adequate time and facilities to prepare a defense but did not have the right to free interpretation.

Although the law requires trials be held within a set time, there were millions of backlogged cases at state, federal, and appellate courts, and courts often took many years to be concluded. To reduce the backlog, state and federal courts frequently dismissed old cases without a hearing. While the law provides for the right to counsel, the Ministry of Justice and Citizenship stated many prisoners could not afford an attorney. The court must furnish a public defender or private attorney at public expense in such cases, but staffing deficits persisted in all states.

Political Prisoners and Detainees

There were no reports of political prisoners or detainees.

Civil Judicial Procedures and Remedies

Citizens may submit lawsuits before the courts for human rights violations. While the justice system provides for an independent civil judiciary, courts were burdened with backlogs and sometimes subject to corruption, political influence, and indirect intimidation. Cases involving violations of an individual's human rights may be submitted through petitions by individuals or organizations to the Inter-American Commission on Human Rights, which in turn may submit the case to the Inter-American Court of Human Rights.

Property Restitution

The law requires proportionate and timely restitution or compensation for governmental takings of private property. Rio de Janeiro NGOs nevertheless reported squatters' rights were not always respected when Rio de Janeiro municipal authorities relocated residents as part of efforts to improve urban mobility and safety in conjunction with the city's Olympic preparations. According to local NGOs, authorities used eminent domain-type laws to relocate approximately 20,000 families, most of whom lacked a legal title to the properties they occupied. Activists and residents argued many of these removals were unnecessary and were carried out mainly to increase property values. Removals in Vila Autodromo, adjacent to the Olympic Park, were cited as examples of such removals. Some residents reported being pressured to accept inadequate compensation for their property.

f. Arbitrary or Unlawful Interference with Privacy, Family, Home, or Correspondence

Although the law and constitution prohibit such actions, NGOs reported police occasionally conducted searches without warrants. Human rights groups, other NGOs, and media reported incidents of excessive police searches in poor neighborhoods. During these operations police stopped and questioned persons and searched cars, residences, and business establishments without warrants.

Section 2. Respect for Civil Liberties, Including:

a. Freedom of Speech and Press

The constitution and law provide for freedom of speech and press, and the government generally respected these rights. Independent media were active and expressed a wide variety of views with minimal restriction, but nongovernmental criminal elements subjected journalists to violence because of their professional activities. Despite national laws prohibiting politically motivated judicial censorship, some local-level courts engaged in judicial censorship. NGOs highlighted instances of violence against journalists. Most were perpetrated by protesters or provocateurs in the context of massive demonstrations, but at times security forces injured journalists during crowd-control operations.

<u>Violence and Harassment</u>: Journalists were sometimes subject to harassment and physical attacks as a result of their reporting. According to Reporters without Borders, four journalists were killed in the country through September. On August 16, Mauricio Campos Rosa, owner of the newspaper *O Grito*, was killed in Belo Horizonte, the state capital of Minas Gerais. According to a local radio station, the

motive was likely related to Rosa's journalistic investigations into corruption involving city councilors and a cooperative responsible for garbage collection.

In February the newspaper *Gazeta do Povo*, based in the state of Parana, published a list of "super salaries" containing the names of judges, public prosecutors, and civil servants who earned more than the maximum salary allowed by law when government benefits were included in the calculation. In response judges and public prosecutors in Parana initiated 37 lawsuits against the newspaper and its employees. In July, Supreme Court Justice Carmen Lucia suspended the lawsuit spending a decision on the proper jurisdiction for the cases. The NGO Committee to Protect Journalists denounced the lawsuits as "judicial harassment."

Internet Freedom

The government did not restrict or disrupt access to the internet or systematically censor online content, and there were no credible reports the government monitored private online communications without appropriate legal authority.

In theory the 2014 landmark Marco Civil law--considered an internet "bill of rights"--enshrines net neutrality and freedom of expression online and provides for the inviolability and secrecy of user communications online, permitting exceptions only by court order. Several legal and judicial rulings citing Marco Civil nevertheless had the potential to threaten freedom of expression on the internet. Anonymous speech is explicitly excluded from constitutional protection, which left little privacy protection for those who used the internet anonymously through a pseudonym. Police and prosecutors may obtain data pursuant to three main statutes: the Wiretapping Act, the Secrecy of Financial Data Act, and the Money Laundering Act.

Private individuals and official bodies took legal action against internet service providers and providers of online social media platforms, such as Google and Facebook, holding them accountable for content posted to or provided by users of the platform. During the year there were at least three instances of messaging applications such as WhatsApp being temporarily blocked for users throughout the country due to judicial decisions related to criminal investigations. A Supreme Federal Court judge overturned the WhatsApp shutdown within hours, citing it as a violation of the constitutional right to freedom of speech.

The electoral law regulates political campaign activity on the internet. The law prohibits paid political advertising online and in traditional media. During the three months prior to an election, the law also prohibits online and traditional media from promoting candidates and distributing content that ridicules or could offend a candidate.

According to CGI.br, the country's internet management committee, 51 percent of households had access to the internet in 2015 and 58 percent of the population used the internet. The government promoted digital inclusion by providing free satellite internet access to remote areas; broadband access to municipal governments, schools, and health centers; computers to selected populations; and other assistance targeting vulnerable communities.

Academic Freedom and Cultural Events

There were no government restrictions on academic freedom or cultural events.

b. Freedom of Peaceful Assembly and Association

The law provides for the freedoms of assembly and association, and the government generally respected these rights.

Freedom of Assembly

The government generally respected rights of freedom of assembly, but police occasionally intervened in citizen protests. In January in the city of Sao Paulo, for instance, military police used tear gas and stun grenades to keep Free Pass Movement (MPL) protesters opposing increases in bus and transit fares from marching on one of the city's main thoroughfares. Local authorities stated MPL leaders had not informed police of the planned route of the march, and therefore police took action to prevent protesters from damaging property, such as banks that were vandalized in previous protests. NGOs reported both the police and MPL played a part in the escalation of events. Some noted police were not consistent in informing demonstrators how far in advance notification of the protest march was required; others noted that during the demonstrations the MPL had tolerated violence perpetrated by groups not affiliated with their organization.

There were a series of large-scale, national protests in March, April, and August calling for the impeachment of President Rousseff and an end to corruption. Police reported no serious security incidents during these protests.

Freedom of Association

The law provides for this right, the government generally respected it.

c. Freedom of Religion

See the Department of State's *International Religious Freedom Report* at
www.state.gov/religiousfreedomreport/.

d. Freedom of Movement, Internally Displaced Persons, Protection of Refugees, and Stateless Persons

The constitution provides for freedom of internal movement, foreign travel, emigration, and repatriation, and the government generally respected these rights. The National Committee for Refugees cooperated with the Office of the UN High Commissioner for Refugees and other humanitarian organizations in providing protection and assistance to refugees, asylum seekers, and other persons of concern.

Protection of Refugees

Access to Asylum: The law provides for the granting of asylum or refugee status, and the government has established a system for providing protection to refugees. By law refugees are provided official documentation, access to legal protection, and access to public services.

Temporary Protection: The government provided assistance to Haitian migrants who entered the country in hope of securing employment and relief from economic conditions in Haiti. To reduce the number of Haitians seeking to enter Brazil via dangerous irregular migration routes, the government extended through October 2017 its policy of issuing humanitarian visas through its embassy in Haiti. The visas entitle the recipients to receive health care and social assistance and grant them the right to work. According to the government, 85,000 Haitian migrants had migrated to the country since 2012.

Section 3. Freedom to Participate in the Political Process

The law provides citizens the ability to choose their government in free and fair periodic elections held by secret ballot and based on universal and equal suffrage.

Elections and Political Participation

Recent Elections: In national elections held in 2014, Dilma Rousseff won a second four-year term as president. Observers considered the elections free and fair. On August 31, congress impeached Rousseff for having violated budget laws, and Vice President Michel Temer assumed the presidency as required by the constitution.

In October voters participated in nationwide municipal elections widely considered free and fair. In the period preceding the municipal elections, however, the Superior Electoral Court and federal police reported that as many as 20 candidates or politicians were killed in violence attributed to organized crime networks. Fifteen of the killings occurred in Rio de Janeiro State, and one high-profile incident occurred in the state of Goias, when the candidate for mayor, Jose Gomes da Rocha, was shot and killed while campaigning. In response to the rise in violence, the federal government deployed tens of thousands of troops to more than 400 municipalities to increase security and guard the transport of ballot boxes and the voting stations. There were no reports of violence on election day.

Participation of Women and Minorities: No laws limit participation of women and minorities in the political process. According to the Secretariat of Women's Policies, women made up 9 percent of national-level legislators in congress, and persons of African descent made up 8.5 percent.

Section 4. Corruption and Lack of Transparency in Government

The law provides criminal penalties for conviction of official corruption and stipulates civil penalties for corruption committed by Brazilians or Brazilian entities overseas, but the government did not always implement the law effectively. There were numerous reports of government corruption, and delays in judicial proceedings against those accused of corruption often resulted in de facto impunity for those responsible. In response to a series of high-profile corruption investigations, millions of citizens participated in anticorruption street protests throughout the country during the year.

Corruption: The investigation of the Petrobras state oil company embezzlement scandal (Operation Carwash, or "Lava Jato"), which began in 2014, continued and led to arrests and convictions of money launderers and major construction contractors, and to the investigation, indictment, and conviction of politicians across the political class. Information gained through collaboration and plea bargains with suspects launched a widening net of new investigations. In September federal investigators executed more than 100 search warrants and froze 8.75 billion reais ($2.5 billion) in four of the largest state-run pension funds in an operation called Operation Greenfield. There were also parallel corruption investigations at the federal and state levels that indicated greater anticorruption scrutiny, ranging from federal parastatal entities to contracts with local governments.

Financial Disclosure: Public officials are subject to financial disclosure laws, and officials generally complied with these provisions. Asset declarations are not made public, but federal employees' salaries and payment information are posted online and can be searched by name.

Public Access to Information: The law provides for public access to unclassified government information. The list of exceptions is sufficiently narrow and includes personal information; information that affects public safety or health, national security, or international relations; and sensitive military and intelligence information. The only fees charged are the costs of printing, copying, and mailing documentation. The government has 20 days to respond to requests and may request an additional 10 days, for a maximum of 30 days, after receiving the request.

Section 5. Governmental Attitude Regarding International and Nongovernmental Investigation of Alleged Violations of Human Rights

A number of domestic and international human rights groups generally operated without government restriction, investigating and publishing their findings on human rights cases. Federal officials were cooperative and responsive to their views. Federal and state officials in many cases sought the aid and cooperation of domestic and international NGOs in addressing human rights problems.

Government Human Rights Bodies: In May a ministerial reform resulted in a restructuring in the composition of numerous federal ministries. The Ministry of Justice and Citizenship was created, which absorbed the competencies of the Secretariat of Women's Policies, Secretariat of Human Rights, and Secretariat of Policies for the Promotion of Racial Equality. Local human rights organizations criticized the reform, since several of these secretariats previously held the rank of ministry and had more autonomy.

The Chamber of Deputies and the Senate had human rights committees that operated without interference and participated in several activities nationwide in coordination with domestic and international human rights organizations. Most states had police ombudsmen, but their accomplishments varied, depending on such factors as funding and outside political pressure.

A National Council for Human Rights, composed of 22 members--11 from various government agencies and 11 from civil society--met regularly. Other councils using this mixed government and civil society model included the National LGBT Council, National Council for Religious Freedom, National Council for Racial Equality Policies, National Council for Rights of Children and Adolescents, and National Council for Refugees.

Section 6. Discrimination, Societal Abuses, and Trafficking in Persons

Women

<u>Rape and Domestic Violence</u>: The law criminalizes rape, including spousal rape. Intimate partner violence remained both widespread and underreported to authorities, due to fear of retribution, further violence, and social stigma. Persons convicted of killing a woman or girl in cases of domestic violence may be sentenced to 12 to 30 years in prison. Longer sentences may be set for conviction of killing a pregnant woman, girls under age 14, or women with disabilities or who are over age 60. According to the Rio de Janeiro Court of Justice's Observatory of Violence Against Women, from January to June 58,000 new cases of violence against women were brought to trial in the state. In May a high-profile case of an adolescent girl's gang rape by 33 individuals ignited a debate regarding the prevalence of gender-based violence. According to UN Women and the Secretariat of Women's Policies, in 2013 an average of 13 women were killed per day in the country due to this type of violence.

The federal government maintained a toll-free nationwide hotline for women to report instances of intimate partner violence (Dial 180). The hotline has the authority to mobilize military police units to respond to such reports and to follow up regarding the status of the case.

Each state secretariat for public security operated police stations dedicated exclusively to addressing crimes against women, which remained a significant problem. The specialized stations provided psychological counseling, temporary shelter, and hospital treatment for survivors of intimate partner violence, including rape, as well as criminal prosecution assistance by investigating incidents and forwarding evidence to courts. State and local governments also operated reference centers and temporary women's shelters. The Brazilian Institute of Geography and Statistics (IBGE) reported 8 percent of municipalities had a dedicated space for the protection and care of victims of gender-based violence.

The law requires health facilities to contact police regarding cases in which a woman was harmed physically, sexually, or psychologically and to collect evidence and statements should the victim decide to prosecute.

Sexual Harassment: Sexual harassment is a criminal offense, punishable by up to two years in prison if convicted. The law prohibits sexual advances in the workplace or educational institutions and between service providers or clients. In the workplace it applies only in hierarchical situations where the harasser is of higher rank or position than the victim. NGOs reported sexual harassment remained a serious concern, particularly because 70 percent of victims were minors.

Reproductive Rights: Couples and individuals have the right to decide the number, spacing, and timing of children; manage their reproductive health; and have access to the information and means to do so, free from discrimination, coercion, or violence.

Discrimination: The law provides for the same legal status and rights for women as for men. According to the Institute of Applied Economic Research, in 2014 women received 70 percent of what men received for equal work.

Children

Birth Registration: Citizenship is derived from birth in the country or from a parent. The National Council of Justice, in partnership with the Secretariat of Human Rights (SDH), acted to reduce the number of children without birth certificates by registering children born in maternity wards. The National Documentation of Rural Workers initiative offered assistance in obtaining birth certificates and other documents for children born in rural areas. In December 2015 the federal government announced the percentage of children without a birth certificate declined to 1 percent.

Child Abuse: Abuse and neglect of children and adolescents were problems. Children and adolescents were victims of rape and molestation, including girls impregnated by family members. The SDH oversaw a program that established nationwide strategies for combating child sexual abuse and best practices for treating victims. The government maintained a protection program for children and adolescents. Sixty percent of the children in the program had received death threats due to involvement in drug trafficking, and most entered the program accompanied by one or more family members. The program offered psychological counseling and technical courses to reinsert these youth into stable community situations.

Early and Forced Marriage: The legal minimum age of marriage is 18 (age 16 with parental or legal representative consent). According to data from the UN Children's Fund, 11 percent of women ages 20-24 were married before age 15, and 36 percent of women ages 20-24 were married before age 18.

Sexual Exploitation of Children: Sexual exploitation of children, adolescents, and other vulnerable persons is punishable by four to 10 years in prison if convicted. The law defines sexual exploitation as prostitution of children, sexual activity, production of child pornography, and public or private sex shows. The law sets a minimum age of 14 for consensual sex, with the penalty for conviction of statutory rape ranging from eight to 15 years in prison.

While no specific laws address child sex tourism, it is punishable under other criminal offenses. The country was a destination for child sex tourism. Several major coastal cities in the Northeast were tourist destinations for the trafficking of children and adolescents for the purpose of commercial sexual exploitation. Additionally, reports indicated sexual exploitation of children and adolescents increased around major construction projects.

The law criminalizes child pornography. The penalty for conviction of possession of child pornography is up to four years in prison and a fine.

The Ministry of Tourism promoted its code of conduct to prevent the commercial sexual exploitation of children in the tourism industry. The Federal Highway Police and the International Labor Organization disseminated awareness materials in places such as gas stations, bars, restaurants, motels, and nightclubs along highways considered areas for sexual exploitation of children and adolescents.

International Child Abductions: The country is a party to the 1980 Hague Convention on the Civil Aspects of International Child Abduction. See the

Department of State's *Annual Report on International Parental Child Abduction* at travel.state.gov/content/childabduction/en/legal/compliance.html.

Anti-Semitism

According to the Jewish Federation, there were approximately 120,000 Jewish citizens, of whom approximately 50,000 were in the state of Sao Paulo and 25,000 in Rio de Janeiro State. It is illegal to write, edit, publish, or sell books that promote anti-Semitism or racism. The law enables courts to fine or imprison anyone who displays, distributes, or broadcasts anti-Semitic materials and for those convicted mandates a two- to five-year prison term.

Several leaders of the Jewish and interfaith communities stated overt anti-Semitism remained limited. According to local reports, Casa Mafalda, an autonomous space for culture and politics in the city of Sao Paulo, was targeted by a neo-Nazi group who painted a swastika on the entrance gate of the institution and wrote references to Hitler. Neo-Nazi groups operated in the southern states of Rio Grande do Sul, Santa Catarina, and Parana.

Trafficking in Persons

See the Department of State's *Trafficking in Persons Report* at www.state.gov/j/tip/rls/tiprpt/.

Persons with Disabilities

The law prohibits discrimination against persons with physical and mental disabilities in employment, air travel and other transportation, education, the judicial system, and access to health care, and the federal government generally enforced these provisions. While federal and state laws mandate access to buildings for persons with disabilities, states did not enforce them effectively.

The Brazilian Inclusion of Persons with Disabilities Act, a legal framework on the rights of persons with disabilities, seeks to promote greater accessibility through expanded federal oversight of the Statute of Cities, harsher criminal penalties for conviction of discrimination based on disability, and inclusive health services with provision of services near residences and rural areas.

The National Council for the Rights of Persons with Disabilities and the National Council for the Rights of the Elderly have primary responsibility for promoting the rights of persons with disabilities. According to the SDH, specific problems included the short supply of affordable and up-to-date orthotics and prosthetics, scarcity of affordable housing with special adaptations, and a need for greater accessibility to public transport. Children with disabilities attended primary and secondary schools and higher educational institutions, but there was a shortage of schools with adequate support. The lack of accessible infrastructure and schools significantly limited the ability of persons with disabilities to participate in the workforce.

Civil society organizations acknowledged that monitoring and enforcement of disability policies remained weak, and criticized a lack of accessibility to public transportation, weak application of employment quotas, and a limited medical-based definition of disability that often excludes learning disabilities. The government improved access for persons with disabilities in its infrastructure development and in retrofitting public sports venues to prepare for sporting events such as the 2016 Paralympic Games.

National/Racial/Ethnic Minorities

The law prohibits racial discrimination, specifically the denial of public or private facilities, employment, or housing, to anyone based on race. The law also prohibits the incitement of racial discrimination or prejudice and the dissemination of racially offensive symbols and epithets, and it stipulates prison terms for such acts.

The 2010 census reported that for the first time white persons constituted less than half the population; approximately 52 percent of the population identified themselves as belonging to categories other than white. Despite this high representation within the general population, darker-skinned citizens, particularly Afro-Brazilians, frequently encountered discrimination.

Afro-Brazilians were underrepresented in the government, professional positions, and middle and upper classes. They experienced a higher rate of unemployment and earned average wages below those of whites in similar positions. There was also a sizeable education gap. Afro-Brazilians were disproportionately affected by crime; according to one congressional investigative report, black men were 3.7 times more likely to be homicide victims than their white counterparts.

The 2010 Racial Equality Statute continued to be controversial, due to its provision for nonquota affirmative action policies in education and employment. In 2012 the

Supreme Court upheld the constitutionality of racial quota systems at universities. A quotas law went into effect that gave the 59 federal universities four years to provide for half of the students of incoming classes to be from public schools, which generally enrolled a higher percentage of Afro-Brazilian students than did private schools. The 2010 law requires 20 percent of federal public administration positions be filled by Afro-Brazilians. The states of Rio de Janeiro, Rio Grande do Sul, Parana, and Mato Grosso do Sul have similar laws for local public administration positions. In August the Ministry of Planning established a requirement for government ministries to set up internal committees to validate the self-declared ethnicity claims of public-service job applicants by using phenotypic criteria, essentially assessing "blackness" in an attempt to reduce abuse of affirmative action policy and related laws.

Indigenous People

According to data from the National Indigenous Foundation (FUNAI) and the 2010 census, there were approximately 896,900 indigenous persons, representing 305 distinct indigenous ethnic groups and speaking 274 distinct languages. The law grants the indigenous population broad protection of their cultural patrimony, exclusive use of their traditional lands, and exclusive beneficial use of their territory. Congress must consult with the tribes involved when considering requests to exploit mineral and water resources, including ones with energy potential, on indigenous lands. The law grants indigenous tribes rights to a portion of the profit resulting from mining. According to the constitution, all aboveground and underground mincrals as well as hydroelectric-power potential belong to the government. FUNAI has a mandated role for an indigenous consultation process, but human rights groups expressed concerns that most of the requirements for indigenous consultation remained unmet and that the body's budget was significantly cut during the year.

Illegal logging, drug trafficking, and mining, as well as changes in the environment from large infrastructure projects, forced indigenous tribes to move to new areas or make their demarcated indigenous territories smaller than established by law.

According to FUNAI, the federal government established rules for providing financial compensation following the occupation in good faith of indigenous areas, as in the cases of companies that won development contracts affecting indigenous lands. Various indigenous peoples protested the slow pace of land demarcations.

The latest report (2015) of the Indigenous Missionary Council cited data from the Special Secretariat for Indigenous Health showing 137 indigenous persons were killed across the country. The council's own research separately found 54 killings of indigenous persons throughout the country. In June public health worker Clodiodi Aquileu Rodrigues de Souza was shot and killed and six indigenous persons were injured in the municipality of Carapo in the state of Mato Grosso do Sul, on land claimed by the Guarani Kaiowa indigenous group. Paramilitary forces acting on instructions of wealthy land owners allegedly carried out the attack as a reprisal against the indigenous community for seeking recognition of their land rights.

Acts of Violence, Discrimination, and Other Abuses Based on Sexual Orientation and Gender Identity

Federal law does not prohibit discrimination based on sexual orientation, but several states and municipalities have administrative regulations that prohibit such discrimination and provide for equal access to government services. Social discrimination remained a problem, especially against the transgender population. Violence against lesbian, gay, bisexual, transgender, and intersex (LGBTI) individuals was a serious concern, with local NGOs reporting that as of June, 139 LGBTI persons were victims of hate killings.

The criminal code states offenses subject to criminal prosecution fall under federal statutes, leaving hate crimes subject to administrative, not criminal penalties. Sao Paulo is the only state to codify punishments for hate-motivated violence and speech against LGBTI individuals. In the state of Rio de Janeiro, the law penalizes commercial establishments that discriminate on grounds of sexual orientation. Sanctions vary from warnings and fines to the temporary suspension or termination of a business license. Fines may reach 15,600 reais ($4,460).

On July 2, Diego Vieira Machado, a student at the Federal University of Rio de Janeiro, was found dead at the Fundao campus, located in the northern region of Rio de Janeiro. His body was partially naked and showed signs of abuse. Friends alleged that the fact he was gay, black, poor, and born in the north of the country clearly played a role. They also said Machado had received several threats prior to the attack.

The National LGBT Council, composed of civil society and government agencies, combated discrimination and promoted the rights of LGBTI persons. Meetings were open to the public and broadcast over the internet.

HIV and AIDS Social Stigma

Discrimination against persons with HIV/AIDS is punishable if convicted by up to four years in prison and a fine. Civil society organizations and the press reported discrimination against persons with HIV/AIDS. According to the UN Program on HIV/AIDS in Brazil, discrimination against certain groups, particularly gay men, made individuals hesitate to seek HIV testing and treatment.

Other Societal Violence or Discrimination

According to the Catholic NGO Pastoral Land Commission, rural violence, death threats, and killings of environmentalists continued to take place. A commission press release cited 47 such killings of environmentalists through September. Global Witness reported 50 killings of environmental activists in 2015 (with 90 percent occurring in the states of Maranhao, Para, and Rondonia).

In October Luiz Araujo, the environmental and tourism secretary of the city of Altamira in the state of Para, was shot and killed in his driveway. Media outlets reported it appeared to be a targeted killing, and an associate of Araujo said he was under pressure because of his efforts against illegal deforestation.

The Brazilian Committee of Human Rights Defenders also reported that in the first four months of the year, 24 human rights defenders were killed, 21 of whom were from organizations that defended land rights.

Section 7. Worker Rights

a. Freedom of Association and the Right to Collective Bargaining

The law provides for freedom of association for all workers (except members of the military, uniformed police, and firefighters), the right with some restrictions to bargain collectively, and the right to strike. The law limits organizing at the enterprise level and imposes a mandatory union tax on workers and employers. By law the armed forces, military police, or firefighters may not strike. Civil police may strike and did so during the year. The law prohibits antiunion discrimination, including the dismissal of employees who are candidates for, or holders of, union leadership positions, and it requires employers to reinstate workers fired for union activity.

New unions must register with the Ministry of Labor, which accepts the registration unless objections are filed by other unions. The law stipulates certain restrictions, such as "unicidade" (in essence one union per city), which limits freedom of association by prohibiting multiple, competing unions of the same professional category in a single geographical area. Unions that represent workers in the same geographical area and professional category may contest registration.

The law stipulates a strike may be ruled "disruptive" by the labor court, and the union may be subjected to legal penalties if the strike violates certain conditions, such as if the union fails to maintain essential services during a strike, notify employers at least 48 hours before the beginning of a walkout, or end a strike after a labor court decision. Employers may not hire substitute workers during a legal strike or fire workers for strike-related activity, provided the strike is not ruled abusive.

The law obliges a union to negotiate on behalf of all registered workers in the professional category and geographical area it represents, regardless of whether an employee pays voluntary membership dues. The law permits the government to reject clauses of collective bargaining agreements that conflict with government policy. Collective bargaining is effectively prohibited in the public sector; the constitution allows it, but as of the end of November implementing legislation had not been enacted.

Freedom of association and the right to collective bargaining were generally respected. Collective bargaining was widespread in establishments in the private sector. Worker organizations were independent of the government and political parties. Cases of intimidation and killings of rural union organizers were reported. In February Francisca das Chagas Silva, a rural social worker from the Mirando do Norte union, was killed after an act of sexual violence. She had played an active part in the Trade Union Study Group (GES Women) and other activities organized by the Rural Workers Trade Union Movement in 2015.

b. Prohibition of Forced or Compulsory Labor

The law prohibits what it calls "slave labor," defined as "reducing someone to a condition analogous to slavery," including subjecting someone to forced labor or exploitative working conditions in general, such as long workdays, unhygienic work conditions, extremely arduous labor, and labor performed in degrading working conditions. While not all individuals in forced labor, as defined by the country's law, were victims of trafficking for the purpose of labor exploitation, many were. The government took a number of actions to enforce the law, although forced labor occurred in a number of states. Violations of forced labor laws are punishable by up to eight years in prison, but this was often not sufficient to deter violations. The law also provides penalties for various crimes related to forced labor, such as illegal recruiting or transporting workers or imposing onerous debt burdens as a condition of employment.

The National Commission to Eradicate Slave Labor coordinated government efforts to combat forced and exploitative labor and provide a forum for input from civil society. The commission's members included representatives from 10 government agencies or ministries--including Human Rights, Justice, Federal Police, Agriculture, Labor, and Environment--and 20 civil society groups. The International Labor Organization was also a member.

The Ministry of Labor's Mobile Inspection Unit teams conducted surprise inspections of properties on which forced labor was suspected or reported, using teams composed of labor inspectors, labor prosecutors from the Federal Labor Prosecutor's Office, and federal police officers. Mobile teams levied fines on landowners who used forced labor and required employers to provide back pay and benefits to workers before returning the workers to their municipalities of origin. Labor inspectors and prosecutors, however, could only apply civil penalties; consequently, many cases were not criminally prosecuted. Workers removed by mobile units were entitled to three months' salary at the minimum wage. State governments in Mato Grosso, Bahia, Rio de Janeiro, and the "Bico do Papagaio" region of the state of Tocantins provided funds to a program that offered vocational training to rescued slave laborers. As of October in the state of Mato Grosso alone, rescued workers received 1.1 million reais ($314,000).

In July labor inspectors rescued two Chinese citizens who were victims of forced labor conditions in a snack bar in Rio de Janeiro.

Forced labor, including forced child labor, occurred in many states in jobs such as clearing forests to provide cattle pastureland, logging, producing charcoal, raising livestock, and other agricultural activities. Forced labor often involved young men drawn from the less-developed northeastern states--Maranhao, Piaui, Tocantins, and Ceara--and the central state of Goias to work in the northern and central-western regions of the country. In addition there were reports of forced labor in the construction industry also involving young men mainly from the Northeast. Cases of forced labor were also reported in the garment industry in the city of Sao

Paulo; the victims were often from neighboring countries, particularly Bolivia, Peru, and Paraguay, while others came from Haiti, South Korea, and China.

Also see the Department of State's *Trafficking in Persons Report* at www.state.gov/j/tip/rls/tiprpt/.

c. Prohibition of Child Labor and Minimum Age for Employment

The minimum working age is 16, and apprenticeships may begin at age 14. The law bars all minors under age 18 from work that constitutes a physical strain or occurs in unhealthy, dangerous, or morally harmful conditions. Hazardous work includes an extensive list of activities within 13 occupational categories, including domestic service, garbage scavenging, and fertilizer production. The law requires parental permission for minors to work as apprentices.

According to the Ministry of Labor, in the last two decades, the number of underage working children declined from eight million to 2.7 million. The cases that remained were the most difficult to identify because they often took place in inaccessible rural areas or within a family home.

The Ministry of Labor is responsible for inspecting worksites to enforce child labor laws. Penalties for violations range from 402 reais to 1,891 reais ($115 to $540), doubling for a second violation and tripling for a third, and were generally enforced; however, observers asserted fines were usually too small to serve as an effective deterrent. Most inspections of children in the workplace were driven by complaints brought by workers, teachers, unions, NGOs, and the media. Due to legal restrictions, labor inspectors remained unable to enter private homes and farms, where much of the child labor occurred.

In May a study published by a Sao Paulo-based foundation devoted to the protection of children's rights (Abrinq Foundation) found that 3.3 million children and adolescents (ages 5-17) were in a situation of child labor. The Ministry of Labor's National Committee for the Eradication of Child Labor continued to implement the country's National Plan to Combat Child Labor and maintained a database on the worst forms of child labor occurring in the country. The government's Mobile Inspection Unit to combat child labor--modeled on the forced-labor Mobile Inspection Unit in place since 1995--continued to expand its operations.

Also see the Department of Labor's *Findings on the Worst Forms of Child Labor* at www.dol.gov/ilab/reports/child-labor/findings/.

d. Discrimination with Respect to Employment and Occupation

Labor laws and regulations prohibit discrimination on the basis of race, sex, gender, disability, religion, political opinion, natural origin or citizenship, age, language, and sexual orientation or gender identity. Discrimination against individuals who are HIV positive or suffer from other communicable diseases is also prohibited. The government generally enforced these laws and regulations, although discrimination in employment occurred with respect to Afro-Brazilians, women, persons with disabilities, indigenous persons, and transgender individuals. The Ministry of Labor implemented rules to integrate promotion of racial equality in its programs, including requiring that race be included in data for programs financed by the ministry, including unemployment insurance.

According to local NGO Reporter Brasil, Haitian workers reported being victims of employment discrimination. The Ministry of Labor published and distributed a workers' rights manual in Portuguese and Haitian Creole, but workers--especially in the construction business--complained some employers displayed racist behavior and would not disclose the rights Haitians had under law, including social security benefits.

e. Acceptable Conditions of Work

In January the national minimum wage increased to 880 reais ($250) per month. According to 2016 IBGE data, the per capita income of approximately 40 percent of workers was below the minimum wage. IBGE data also revealed 6.8 percent of workers (12.9 million) were considered "extremely poor" or earning less than 70 reais ($20) per month.

The law limits the workweek to 44 hours and specifies a weekly rest period of 24 consecutive hours, preferably on Sundays. The law also provides for paid annual vacation, prohibits excessive compulsory overtime, limits overtime to two hours per workday, and stipulates that hours worked above the monthly limit must be compensated with at least time-and-a-half pay; these provisions generally were enforced for all groups of workers in the formal sector. The constitution also provides for the right of domestic workers to an eight-hour workday, a maximum of 44 hours' work per week, a minimum wage, a lunch break, social security, and severance pay. According to IBGE, 39 percent of workers were employed in the informal sector in 2015.

The Ministry of Labor sets occupational, health, and safety standards that are consistent with internationally recognized norms, although unsafe working conditions were prevalent throughout the country, especially in construction. The law requires employers to establish internal committees for accident prevention in workplaces. It also provides for the protection of employees from being fired for their committee activities. Workers could generally remove themselves from situations that endangered their health or safety without jeopardy to their employment, although those in forced labor situations without access to transportation were particularly vulnerable to situations that endangered their health and safety.

In July local NGOs reported violation of workers' rights, workplace accidents, and long work days in the food production and cattle industry across several states, including Sao Paulo and Santa Catarina. One truck driver reported being required to drive for 20 hours per day, from Sunday to Sunday. On November 28, an explosion occurred at an insecticide factory in the municipality of Diadema in the state of Sao Paulo, injuring at least 16 persons, including firefighters. According to local authorities, the factory had no environmental license.

The Ministry of Labor addressed problems related to acceptable conditions of work such as long workdays and unsafe or unhygienic work conditions. Penalties for violations include fines that varied widely depending on the nature of the violation; the fines were generally enforced and were sometimes sufficient to deter violations. The National Labor Inspection School held various training sessions for labor inspectors throughout the year. The Ministry of Labor reported the number of labor inspectors (2,500) in the country was insufficient to enforce full compliance nationwide.